POOLE
THEN & NO

HARRY ASHLEY

COUNTRYSIDE BOOKS
NEWBURY, BERKSHIRE

First Published 1991

COUNTRYSIDE BOOKS
3 CATHERINE ROAD
NEWBURY, BERKSHIRE

ISBN 1 85306 164 6

Produced through MRM Associates Ltd., Reading
Typeset by Acorn Bookwork, Salisbury
Printed in England by J.W. Arrowsmith Ltd., Bristol

CONTENTS

To John Hillier and the Poole Historical Trust.
A thank you for the pleasure their books gave me.

ACKNOWLEDGEMENTS

This pictorial document could only be prepared with the help of people who love Poole as much as I do.

My thanks to Brian Galpin and Ken Gibbs of the Society of Poole Men who let me search through their photographic collections, the Evening Echo, Bournemouth and the librarians who helped me recall pictures I had taken nearly half a century ago. Ian Andrews, Town Clerk of Poole, and Graham Smith, Curator of the Museum, and his painstaking staff helped me fill gaps in this pictorial record of Poole's 30 year revolutionary change from a dour fading port to a prospering go-ahead modern town and a special thank you to Ann Norbury of the Documentation and Research Department of Poole Museum for her patience and assistance in helping me in my picture quest. The book also enables me to fulfil a promise to the late Sidney Batting, Poole Marine photographer, that I would use his historical boating photographs. Thanks also to the Harbour Commissioners and RNLI for the use of photographs.

Finally, once again, I express my pleasure at having had an excuse to delve into the excellent histories of Poole produced by the Poole Historical Trust. John Hillier's team produce in-depth volumes which should have a place on every Poole family's bookshelf.

My publisher, Nicholas Battle, gave me the chance to write this book on the '30 Year Revolution' which I had observed throughout. It has been an absorbing and pleasurable assignment.

INTRODUCTION

Poole Past and Present, the excellent pictorial book from the archives of Poole lecturer and historian, George Blake, made a then and now approach to the Poole scene with locations photographed from similar positions with a gap of about 100 years between pictures.

The Poole of the 1990s did not grow from the ashes of the old. In the early post-war years Poole decided to take on a new image. Vast acres were flattened and cleared to ground level, old properties were razed to the ground and famous little lanes and thoroughfares, some so dark that they had to be whitewashed to give more light, were bulldozed. Many famous locations were obliterated, together with names which were never revived; Pluddie Lane, Rozzer Lane, Fish Shambles and Mud Lane are all now moulded into a new Poole.

The city fathers, well-known for their love of Poole's historic past and publicly declaring their dislike of change, suddenly went berserk and, except for a small area around the Parish Church, preserved in its original style, allowed great areas to be torn down. They bulldozed the very heart of the town, demolishing theatres and hotels, tore down a brewery and literally blew up the gas works. The authorities were also mindful of the hold-ups caused by traffic at the train crossing gates which were in the main High Street and built a modern fly-over road to obviate that problem.

A huge shopping precinct was planned at the town centre which included a bus station, multi-storey car park and sports centre. Adjacent was an Arts Complex with Concert Hall, Cinema and Galleries. For the first time in many years the town stood up with pride and faced the challenge of neighbouring Bournemouth.

The population increased and came near that of the famous seaside resort next door, once in Hampshire but now part of Dorset since the County boundary changes in the 1970s. Important commercial firms, seeing the new Poole growing, decided to set up shop in the ancient port. Barclay International built a dominating building facing the new town centre complex and large insurance concerns made Poole their headquarters. The Royal National Lifeboat Institution not only took over an existing quayside boatyard but built their headquarters administration building nearby. Falkland Square just seemed to fall into the great jigsaw of change, yet it was sited in the old heart of Poole and over long-known thoroughfares. Luckily, here and there a building has resisted demolition to give the only clues to the way it was. The Dolphin Hotel and the George Inn are two examples.

This destruction and rebuilding has taken place in under three decades and author Harry Ashley, former chief photographer of the *Evening Echo*, Bournemouth, recorded the changes, often wondering how the jigsaw of new buildings and car parks would fit together. Those changes are the subject of this book, which shows Poole's progress in pictures. Whilst the new factory areas have brought new prosperity to the town, it is primarily a seaport and its interest will always centre around the dockside with the shipbuilding yards, Cross Channel Ferry services and leisure pursuits.

Poole came out of its long sleep and wears its new bright image of stone moulded into elaborate designs like a young man in a new suit.

The single thoroughfare town with its shabby uninteresting High Street making an almost straight line to the harbour has been replaced by a complex system of new roads and exciting buildings. From some angles it is a city of the future. The authorities must be congratulated on the chance they took, because unlike many cities and coastal ports, Poole was not rebuilding because it had been bombed during the War, but because the authorities realised that the small town lay-out was not in keeping with a leading seaport standing on the shores of one of Europe's most beautiful harbours.

With the ruthless clearance of a working town and eventual rebuilding, Poole has grown in stature. New docks cope with the growing Channel ferry trade, industry has also discovered the town, it leads in artistic and leisure pursuits and even hosts the Bournemouth Symphony Orchestra.

Poole also became conscious of her leisure and tourist capabilities. Because of the large harbour, the town is divorced from its main beaches at Branksome Chine and Sandbanks. These sandy shores now with excellent facilities, car parks and bus services, share the clean waters of Poole Bay with miles of Bournemouth beaches and chines which stretch over 5 miles to Hengistbury Head.

Poole, with a present population of 135,000, is a proud and polished port with a busy tourist trade, several light industry estates and is an important ferry port – a showpiece town, regularly visited by council authorities from all over the country.

Harry W. Ashley

HARRY ASHLEY

OLD POOLE

So vast is the change in the lay-out of Poole that it is difficult to remember the town as it was at the end of the Second World War. Entering from Longfleet the visitor arrived in the wide shopping square formed by the division of the High Street, one road leading to Longfleet and the other forking off to Wimborne. A little further south, Towngate Street joined the main road causing another wide junction. Towngate Street led to the Railway Station. The High Street, narrowing all the way, eventually reached the Town Quay, a typical harbourside with a long quay space and lined with warehouses, seaport inns where you jostled with seafaring characters – blonde men from timber supplying countries, French fishermen in striped jerseys or rust coloured canvas smocks reeking of fish or a Johnny Onion man enjoying an English pint before setting off on a bicycle loaded with strings of gold coloured onions.

A labyrinth of narrow lanes and passageways opening out on the quay formed the lacklustre homes for fishermen and dockworkers. Behind this area was the gas works, a vast complex which spread right up to the town centre. These were two of the areas which were pulled down and with them the giant transporter cranes which lifted the coal from colliers to feed the gas works. This operation on a windy day made life along the quay uncomfortable as the dust was whipped from the buckets. Fishermen's Dock formed the east end of the quay and beyond the mudflats of Baiter had already been reclaimed to form a harbourside park and open space.

Towngate Street, the Ladies' Walking Field and the whole of the shopping area from Foregate Street to the George Hotel, which still exists, had to be lost in the plan to build a fly-over conveying traffic over the railway and accommodating the Bus Station, car parks, shopping centre and Arts & Leisure complexes at the heart of new Poole.

The slow destruction of the old and gradual rebirth of the new Poole spanned more than three decades and those who lived through the change will have forgotten places and incidents over that time. This book will recall places and serve as a permanent reminder of Poole's progress in the 30 year revolution.

This first chapter reminds us of that long forgotten Poole, the alleyways in Old Town, so decrepit that when the houses emptied they soon decayed and fell apart like scabs on an unhealthy body. Ensuing chapters deal with the clearance of these areas, the obliteration of the town generations had known and the emergence of a proud seaport, not a concrete jungle as many thought it would be, but exciting buildings in brick and lovely white stone which is weathering to project a 'Poole of the Future'.

MANY BOOKS have depicted the drab demoralising streets which led off Poole's harbourside. The excellent Poole Historical Trust books have portrayed almost every house. Here is a selection to remind us of Poole's decaying era so that comparisons can be made with the new Poole which emerged in the 1980s. Barber's Piles, (*left*) formerly Barber's Lane, was a typical thoroughfare, a continuation of Thames Street to the West Quay road. The parish church of St James is in the background. Lagland Street (*right*) was one of the wider streets and off it narrower lanes branched. Here is Old Orchard at its junction with Lagland Street. On the left is a gas lamp fixed to the Maltsters Arms public house. This picture was taken shortly before the Second World War.

THE HIGH Street showing Miles, the drapers, right, a building which in the 1870s was the main Post Office. The clock is on the premises of James Cole, the watchmaker. Picture taken about the beginning of the First World War. Note the waiting cart horse.

BETWEEN THE two Great Wars no day out to Sandbanks was complete without a visit to Harvey's Tea Rooms on the harbour shore. The site is now part of the Royal Motor Yacht Club and yachts and cars are now parked on the area where families sat around trestle tables for tea and cake.

LOOKING DOWN Poole High Street over 100 years ago. It shows an early Anstey Arms, right, and no evidence of the railway further down the road. Today this is the site of Falkland Square, which although a precinct is busier than it was as Poole's main thoroughfare in 1884.

THIS RARE thatched cottage in the strange surroundings of the busy High Street survived until 1910 when it was removed and Poole's first Woolworth Store was built on the site. The cottage was 16th century and in the 1890s was the home of Arthur James, the Town Crier, who doubled the task with that of billposter. The clock on the right hand side of the picture is above James Cole's watch-making establishment.

THE CORN Market at the lower end of the High Street. The central building was formerly the ironmongers establishment of George Norton. Later it was taken over by Bacon & Curtis in the 1880s. The bank buildings on the left were built in 1826 for the Poole Bank of Fryer, Andrews & Company and eventually they were taken over by the National Provincial Bank. An area that has changed little over the decades.

ANOTHER OF the Poole lanes which honeycombed the quayside area of the old town, Blue Boar Lane is now mainly built over and only a small courtyard exists from the original lane and can be seen at the quay between the Lord Nelson and The Jolly Sailor inns.

CASTLE STREET, a place of historical interest, with the Rising Sun (circa 1600) centre. It runs from the Quay to the High Street. Here Poole men fought with the Spanish and French in 1405. They were avenging the dire deeds of Poole privateer Harry Page. Later it was known as Bloody Street and eventually Castle Street. Today it is the site of large brick office blocks.

POOLE PARK Boating Lake and you can put your own date because since the 1930s it has changed little. A safe place for children to learn to sail. Many well-known helmsmen took their first lessons on these gentle waters.

THEN AND NOW

The rebuilding of Poole was of course a slow process and it is a tribute to the planners that at the end of the day all the various projects came together like the construction of a giant jig-saw puzzle.

The pictures in the following chapter sometimes compare the old and the new and sometimes show the old in its final hours before demolition. Some streets, important in the life of old Poole, disappeared without trace and now the whole is complete it is impossible to see where some roads were situated.

In Falkland Square bearings can be taken from the familiar frontage of the Dolphin Hotel but as you stand in this enclosed shopping precinct which commemorates the 1982 engagement in the South Atlantic or sit on one of the benches where shoppers meet and gossip, try and recall the days when traffic rolled continuously along this very place until the train gates closed to cause long tail-backs of cars containing infuriated drivers. As the town grew in importance it became obvious that a solution had to be found to this problem and at one time it was talked of raising the train tracks and building a high level station similar to the railway at Worcester which had the same problem. Finally, in the new Poole the planners reversed the idea and built the splendid fly-over bridge for the traffic which looks down on the modern station and feeds roads to the old town, docks and western shore with the aid of a giant roundabout.

The building of the great Barclay International edifice adjacent to the fly-over not only dominated the new complex but was the high spot on the skyline of a fresh looking modern town. The Ladies, Walking Field, not it seems a place of romantic meetings but where ladies walked twisting and plaiting new rope, became the site of a multi-storey car park adjacent to the Arndale phase one and near the Arts Centre. At this point in the final development another road rose up in a new fly-over across the railway to give quick access to Baiter Shore and large new residential areas. In the early 1990s the site of the old gas holder can still be seen as it forms a shallow puddle in rainstorms, but such is the development that four veterans who live there all gave different locations for the main building that comprised the old gas works.

Sandbanks harbour shore has also seen great changes. Once the spit was covered in shacks, old bungalows and a variety of buildings, many of which served as summer holiday homes. Today Sandbanks has a Continental look and is packed with expensive residences. The house-boats which used to lie off-shore have long gone and hundreds of yachts moor at this cove, a convenient place for a quick dash to the sea. The Royal Motor Yacht Club, whose headquarters is at Sandbanks, has its own little harbour adjoining the clubhouse.

THE DEATH throes of Poole's heart. Towngate Street is closed, The Anstey at the far end empty, and a pile of rubble exists where the garden centre displayed plants. The old Conservative Club is glimpsed left and a wall, foreground, seals off the road from the railway. The Gas Works can be seen in the background right. *Inset* shows

part of the Arndale Centre which covers the area to-day with a ramp leading to the car park. Marks & Spencer and other buildings of new Poole seen in the large photograph can be seen at the top. Note the electrification of the railway lines with a third rail.

THE VICTORIAN station had its entrance just beyond the train gates in Towngate Street and on the opposite side of the station approach was the Junction Hotel.

THE NEW station is elegant and very modern with ample car-parking space. Much of the old station's goods yards were used for this purpose.

FURTHER MASS clearance took place at the town centre. The rear of the Dolphin Hotel is prominent and the town's Regent Theatre was one of the last buildings to be demolished. A following picture shows the final demise of the popular Theatre (left) which was mainly a Cinema in its last years.

THE DOLPHIN remains intact with the rear entrance now the frontage. The old front entrance opens on to Falkland Square. The hotel is overshadowed by the circular car park. This view of the modern Poole taken from the fly-over bridge shows the exciting architecture to its full advantage. The great Barclay International edifice dominates the area.

THE LAST days of the Regent Theatre. Burning rubble cloaks what was the only modern building in the High Street. Its foundations are somewhere in the great Arndale (Dolphin) complex. The George Hotel, extreme right, is the only guide as to where the Regent actually stood.

THE OLD heart of Poole. Looking up the High Street toward Longfleet from the Anstey corner. The picture is taken from Towngate Street. The High Street leads off right. The Dolphin Hotel, centre left, is the one building which will remain constant as the changes seen in the next few photographs take place.

THE DATE is 1979. This view, taken from the High Street, shows the second stage of the Arndale (later Dolphin) complex rising which has sealed off the High Street. The building left is the Anstey Inn.

THE NEW Poole. Only the Dolphin Hotel remains. The picture is photographed through the ornamental clocktower in what is now known as Falkland Square, commemorating the part played by Poole Royal Marines in the Falklands conflict. The lady approaching with a pram is walking down the middle of the old High Street.

THE LITTLE backwater of Sterte Bay was a peaceful corner of the upper harbour where gulls drifted on waters which reflected the modern flats. Now that has changed and infilled to carry a fast road from town centre to the main Poole–Dorchester road.

THE NEW fast road follows reclaimed land around the end of the harbour shore. The houses on the right of the photograph, now well inland, were formerly divided from the harbour by a narrow promenade.

TWO LOCAL yacht clubs lay claim to being Poole's oldest. One of them, Poole, started out in this old public house at Hamworthy before the turn of the century. The club, then known as the Hamworthy & Bournemouth Sailing Club, later changed its name to the Poole Yacht Club.

STILL AT Hamworthy, the Poole Yacht Club is now housed in a palatial new club house with its own harbour and deep water up to the club house. It is part of the new development on that shore, principally for Channel Ferries.

THE POOLE Harbour Yacht Club started life in the 1930s as an ordinary proprietary club. Today it is a leading yachting centre with marina and yacht yard repair services.

TODAY THE Salterns Yacht Centre has moorings for hundreds of yachts. The marina section is full of cruisers and sailing yachts which can go to sea any day of the year. International races for the larger classes of sailing yachts are often started from this base.

THE OLD Fish Shambles stood on the quay near the Jolly Sailor Inn and was dispensing fish in 1830. Both this building and a subsequent one have long disappeared. A strange custom allowed fish to be sold from these premises for an hour before it was offered to normal fish shops.

A MODERN shelter built in the 1990s outside the Lord Nelson reminds visitors of the old Fish Shambles.

KINGLAND ROAD which had faced the Ladies' Walking Field for many years is pulled down to make way for the Poole Arts Centre. This was the beginning of the rebuilding of Poole and was all completed before the assault on the town centre started.

THE NEW Poole Arts Centre, pride of the new Poole, houses Theatre, Concert Hall, Cinema, Reception Suites, Bars, Cafes and Workshops. The Concert Hall converts to Ballroom when the raked seating is folded under the stage.

COUNTY GATES in 1917. The boundary between Bournemouth and Poole. The stone gate-post and estate cottage were the entrance to the drive which serviced the Manor House at Branksome Chine. Today it is the main road to Sandbanks Ferry, the gateway to Swanage and the Purbecks.

A LARGE roundabout, office blocks and new roads have obliterated the crossroads where Poole men scowled at their Bournemouth counterparts when they came to beat the bounds. The towns are so tightly linked that it is now impossible to know when you leave one town for the other. Both are now in Dorset.

POOLE FOUNDRY was a gloomy, if important landmark near the parish church of St James near Poole Quay. When Poole fishermen were in lean times they used to dredge up cannon balls from the harbour bed to sell to the Foundry. These shells were fired from practice cannons at Hamworthy towards a target on the tip of Brownsea Island.

THE SITE of the Poole Foundry was cleared in the 1980s and a courtyard of elegant town houses called Barber's Wharf, by Lovell Construction was built around a fountain featuring performing Poole dolphins.

SANDBANKS, ONCE a lonely Poole outpost at the bottom of the harbour, began to develop in the 1920s and houseboats were moored off the harbour shore. The first was an old converted lifeboat. In 1930 the Harbour Board ordered their removal.

SANDBANKS TO-DAY. Flowered rockeries line the road to this Poole playground. The bay inside the harbour, now free of the sand and reed islands, is a popular hunting ground for sail-board enthusiasts. Acres and acres of shallow water. The Sandbanks spit once covered by cheap holiday bungalows and huts, is now one of the most expensive residential areas in the South. Over 30 years ago shore properties were topping £100,000.

ONE OF the early phases of the great Poole redevelopment was the clearing of the Ladies' Walking Field, an open space with football pitches, to commence the building of the Arndale Centre and the multi-storey car park. Kingland Road is on the right. The buildings in the left background are part of the Gas Works.

THE CAR park with Arndale Centre (now Dolphin) behind now fill the Ladies' Walking Field and the Arts Centre is seen right. In the background is the dominating Barclay International building. The old Poole Grammar School building stood in the open land in front of the Arts Centre.

THE SITE clearers attempted to get rid of the Gas Works by blowing up the piles on which it stood but it only toppled to a drunken angle and remained so for about 12 months.

ELEGANT HOUSING estates now stand on land once part of the Pitwines Gas Works. Overhead buckets brought the coal to the retorts from colliers at Poole Quay.

POOLE HAS had lifeboats for many years, long before the RNLI decided to make their Headquarters at the Dorset port. The Harmer, the last rowing boat on station, is seen here leaving Fishermen's Dock. She served Poole from 1910 to 1939; 37 ft. long she carried a crew of 12 to 15 and saved 60 lives.

POOLE'S LIFEBOAT in the 1980s, a sophisticated 44 ft. Waverney boat.

A BUSY scene on the town's Great Quay around the turn of the century. Steam engine and horse-drawn cart are all part of systems used in unloading ships' cargoes, a great deal of it manhandled without use of cranes. On the right behind the cart the old Harbour Offices feature. The chimney belonged to the Iron Foundry.

THE SAME view in the 1990s. Piplers, the ship chandlery business, still survives and the old Harbour Offices are now the home of HM Coastguard. On the right is Thames Street which cut through the town cellars, seen right and built in the early 15th century. It was said to be the longest building in the country at the time. The left hand side is now part of the King Charles Inn.

THE TRANSPORTERS which unloaded coal from the colliers to be carried in overhead buckets over the housetops to Pitwines Gas Works were a feature of the Great Quay. The vessel, a regular caller, was the *William Cash*.

The Gas Works has long ago disappeared, the transporters pulled down and only the black and white building at the right of the photograph remains to remind us of the coal unloading days. On the site now is the exclusive Quay Hotel, one of Poole's leading hotels.

LOOKING UP the High Street from the train crossing gates. The old Electric Theatre is seen near centre right.

THE SAME view in rebuilt Poole. Use of stone, brick and a variety of architectural shapes have prevented the new Poole from becoming a concrete jungle.

HIGH STREET, Longfleet, showing a tram at the beginning of its journey to Bournemouth. The tram service started in 1905 and ran until the middle 1930s.

THE VIEW in 1991. The Square and all the complex of buildings in the new Dolphin Centre have mellowed and become so much part of Poole that most residents have forgotten the scene when it was an uninteresting street leading to the harbour.

THE OLD High Street train gates showing the station on its old site. In the redeveloped Poole the station was moved about 100 yards to allow the fly-over bridge space to carry road traffic over the railway tracks.

THE SAME view today showing part of the Dolphin complex. The building, top left, built in 1991 replaced the old Junction Hotel which dominated the old Station Approach. The new flyover bridge is also seen in the background.

A GLIMPSE of the past before the change of Poole's face was decided. Towngate Street leading to the Station is right and the High Street wends its way left to the Old Town and quays. The train crossing is near the cars seen on left.

THE OLD Anstey, drinking haunt of generations of Poole men has gone. Such names as Coppernob and Cheltenham & Gloucester decorate the shops now part of Falkland Square. In the distance a train is seen crossing the old High Street.

LONGFLEET WHERE the High Street divided, one road leading to Bournemouth and the other to Wimborne and the West. Amongst shops remembered are the Evening Echo office, left, Harker & Curtis and Kennedys. On the right was the old Poole Herald Office and Bourne Radio. The date is 1962 and the picture was taken from the George Hotel.

1991 AND a view from the same bedroom at the George. The transformation is difficult to believe. The Central Library is left and the Dolphin Centre hides Falkland Square. On the right the fly-over and a glimpse of the new modern Railway Station.

BRANKSOME CHINE is one of Poole's coastal leisure centres. A straight, former estate, road runs direct from County Gates at Westbourne. In 1912 its facility was this thatched cabin and there was no promenade.

BRANKSOME CHINE today with beach huts, restaurants and toilet facilities and a large car park. Branksome Dene Chine, Canford Cliffs and Sandbanks are all popular watering places under the control of Poole authorities.

ON THE 23rd March 1918 Frank sent this postcard to his friend in Boscombe. It was the accepted way of making appointments. The horse-drawn cart making its way over the Poole High Street level crossing belonged to the United Yeast Company.

THE SAME view in 1991. Modern Continental-style crossing gates have replaced the old gates and only pedestrians are held up when the trains cross because it is now a precinct.

THE PORT OF POOLE

Poole has one of the world's largest natural harbours and arguably the most beautiful. The small single entrance at Sandbanks, about 400 yards wide, is the only way into a great estuary with 110 miles of coastline, six bays, eight named islands and two towns. It is fed by Dorset rivers, Frome and Piddle, and countless smaller ones from the Purbeck hills. No harbour has a longer or more varied history and Poole only became the leading port when deeper draught vessels could no longer reach the older Saxon port at Wareham.

Ill-feeling between the fishermen of Wareham and Poole caused the Barons of Winchelsea to define Poole's fishing limits in 1365 and presented them with a Charter. The ceremony of Beating those Bounds has been carried out periodically since 1609 and successive generations have adapted the perambulation to suit the era.

The men of Poole are proficient in shipbuilding skills. Stately sailing vessels were built on the harbour shores and later racing yachts. During the Second World War naval ships were constructed at Hamworthy and Poole. The latter yard, Bolsons, then turned their skills to building coasting ships and dredgers and to-day Sunseeker International export Express cruisers at the top of the leisure market, some of them costing hundreds of thousands of pounds, with every conceivable gadget for the owner's comfort and sophisticated navigational aids.

At the beginning of the 19th century the town's prosperity revolved around its trade with Newfoundland. The rich merchants operated 350 ships exporting locally made rope, cordage, sail-cloth and nets as well as clothing. The ships brought home cod, salmon, sealskins and oil. Poole also had a large oyster fleet.

Queen Elizabeth I had made Poole a Corporate and free town and created it 'The County Town of Poole'. That entitled the port to a Sheriff. There was, however, a recession by the middle of the 19th century and only the clay trade kept the port alive. The clay was brought by barges from the Purbecks to the quays. Poole got back on its feet by transporting grain and fuel. Flour mills opened on the quay as well as breweries, and foundries producing lamp-posts and steam engines.

In the 1990s Poole has become a leading ferry port and new docks were built at Hamworthy to accommodate roll-on roll-off ferries, trading with the Channel Islands and the Continent.

The port has played a leading role in wars and in 1944 it was the take-off base for American troops who, in over 300 craft, sailed out on June 5th 1944 to the tragic beaches of Omaha and Utah on D-Day. RAF Sunderland flying boats operated from Poole and BOAC flying boats used the base after the war with aircraft flying in daily from many parts of the world. In the 1990s it is an important base for the Royal Marines and from the yacht clubs, around the shore, 10,000 yachtsmen sail a variety of craft, large and small. The port still has an active fishing fleet and boatloads of amateurs head to sea at weekends to try their skills.

Poole is a lively port with commercial interests, those engaged in leisure pursuits and conservation all playing an active part in enhancing and protecting its future.

POOLE HARBOUR in the days when masts reached to the skies and sail was the accepted propulsion for trading ships. On the left is the paddle steamer *Telegraph*, which ran a service to Swanage, and sometimes towed the rowing lifeboat to sea. She had a clinker built wooden hull.

STEAM WAS making its appearance at the turn of the century. This photograph taken from the same viewpoint at Poole Bridge shows the *Narena* registered at Liverpool.

BLACK SMOKE and steam drift over the harbour as steam takes over from sail. This photograph, probably taken in the 1930s shows tramp steamers and colliers in the background at the Gas Works gantries. The paddle steamer, right, is the Cosen & Company's *Victoria*, based at Weymouth, and the twin-funnelled paddler, left, might be the *Brodick Castle*. Open launches, foreground, are Bolson 'Skylarks'.

TODAY'S YACHTSMEN share the harbour with giant cross-Channel ferries. The large vessels reach the sea via a new main channel cut to give vessels quick passage from Hamworthy. Roll-on roll-off ferries and passenger boats arc in and out of the port 24 hours a day.

LOOKING DOWN harbour the new Poole Yacht Club and haven is featured. Poole Bridge can be seen, left and the newly reclaimed dockland at Hamworthy. The Old Town Quay is above the bridge. Poole Park, Parkstone Bay are top left of photograph. In the far distance, top left, the great hotels of Bournemouth are seen.

A BUSY day at Poole Quay in 1951. Always busy with timber imports the Dutch ship *Noordland* unloads wood. Behind is another timber ship, the French-owned *Nicoya*. In the background, just this side of a collier, is the Cosens' paddle steamer *Embassy*, one of the last in service locally.

A VERY different scene in the 1990s. The main docks are at Hamworthy and the Town Quay is taken over by tourists who come to see a variety of craft calling at the port. The 982 ton roll-on-roll-off ferry is seen astern of the square rigged training ship *Maria Asumpta*. Built in 1858 she is the oldest working sailing ship. Holiday-makers queue for a trip around the harbour.

POOLE HAS built countless fine ships and always kept abreast of the trends. The square-rigged *Waterwitch* built in 1871 at Hamworthy was still working in 1936. She was then bought by an Estonian for £400 and sailed until the end of the Second World War.

BOLSONS, AFTER building Admiralty ships in the Second World War turned to a long programme of ships between 1947 and 1977, including coasters, suction dredgers, tugs and oil rig supply vessels. Job No. 538, a 525 ton dredger *Sand Snipe* at her launching in 1961.

IN THE 1990s a local firm, Sunseeker International, build the ultimate in luxury power cruisers. This latest offering for 1991 is the 50 foot Superhawk. She will set you back over £230,000.

POOLE WAS a pioneer in the sport of powerboating and early races were held between quays, a practice which would not be allowed today. This RMYC regatta race took place in the 1930s.

POWER BOATS had become bigger and more sophisticated by the 1960s. A race off Canford Cliffs in that decade.

SERVICE FLYING boats flew from Poole in the Second World War and BOAC flew its World routes from 1946 until the early 1950s. The air giants at anchor as one of Poole's 20 classes of racing yachts sail by.

POOLE'S SECOND bridge was built in 1885. It served until 1927 when the present bridge was constructed costing £33,591. Now there is a possibility of a road crossing to Hamworthy in Holes Bay.

POOLE'S EXISTING lifting bridge. Nearing the end of its days it causes long traffic hold-ups.

TOP POWERBOAT men have used the waters of Poole Harbour in tests for world records. In the 1930s Hubert Scott Paine caught on fire during speed trials. In 1934 he set up a World Record, obtaining a speed of 110 mph in *Miss Britain III* on a harbour course.

IN 1947 SIR Malcolm Campbell tested his last *Bluebird* in Wareham Channel and at high speed almost ran ashore in the shallows.

THE CEREMONY of Beating the Bounds of Poole harbour as granted by the Barons of Winchelsea in 1365 has been carried out periodically since 1609. Successive generations have varied the style of proceedings according to the times. The ceremony was revived in the 1920s and has been carried out regularly since. Shown here is a strange encounter in the 1920s. Pirates meet Indians in the uppper reaches of the harbour.

THE GREAT parade of Poole craft, including Royal Marines, pirates, harbour officials, yachtsmen and lifeboats, escort the Admiral's barge up the harbour at the end of the day, a colourful and exciting end to a day's perambulation, and crowds lined the Poole Great Quay to watch the pirates captured and made to walk the plank into the harbour. A ceremony in the 1980s.

POOLE TODAY

County Gates, the well-known crossroads on the old Dorset boundary at Westbourne, was for decades the plainly marked division between the two towns. It was here that the old worthies of Poole shook their fists at Bournemouth people when they came to beat their land bounds and if rapidly expanding Bournemouth had decided to make a take-over bid the Poole men would have brought cannons to defend their territory. The destruction of the County Gates which physically were the entrance to Branksome Park estate and its big house, Branksome Towers (later an hotel), and replacing it with a roundabout, confused the Poole men – they could not find the boundary mark and the site of the old stone.

Without ceremony the last remaining pillar of the estate wall was felled in 1991 as another great office block reached to the sky and completed the annihilation of County Gates. It is less important now that Poole and Bournemouth are both part of Dorset and for decades the two have been neatly intertwined and depend on each other, but old feelings die hard and some Poole residents still retain an inferiority complex and refuse to accept the young Bournemouth which has long been world famous.

At the time of the Second World War Poole was deep in one of its depressions but from the 1950s suddenly took a new interest in survival and now proudly in the 1990s has not only reclothed dingy streets with exciting, clean and uniquely designed buildings but replaced shabby little shops with new frontages and leading stores have moved into the shopping precincts. The new Poole also has a Sports Centre, Swimming Pool, Central Library and Arts Centre, all served with large car parks, and is secretly delighted at becoming the home of Bournemouth's famous Symphony Orchestra.

The Bus Station is at the heart of this vast town complex and Poole's new railway station, keeping up the modern theme, would surprise the long dead city fathers who knew the dour Victorian platforms.

Mindful of its great heritage, Poole has preserved its past in four museums housed in ancient buildings which are themselves part of Poole's history. Curator Graham Smith leads a dedicated team and carried out several digs as the old Poole came tumbling down.

Pitwines, the site of the former gasworks, reached from the town centre to the quay and this area already houses a food store, and housing estates are gradually reaching back from the harbourside.

A lot of the old town has been refurbished and sometimes adapted to new purposes. For instance, many old quayside granaries and stores are now restaurants, shops and offices. The wealthy merchants built their mansions in various parts of the town and most of these have been preserved.

Not everyone will like the new image created by the Poole skyline of the Nineties but no-one can deny that the planners have produced a town preparing to become a city. An attractive, clean-looking seaport which is attracting more and more great organisations to set up their headquarters in a go-ahead centre.

POOLE'S ELEGANT Town Quay has become a tourists' centre in the 1990s. With the main ferry trade operating from Hamworthy at self-contained docks where it is easier to maintain security, the warehouses of former trading eras serve as shops, offices and restaurants. The Harbour Commissioners have their control building with a view down the harbour. The old harbour inns are an attraction for visitors. HM Customs which operated from the Georgian building on the quay have also moved across the harbour into an elegant modern building.

OLD AND new buildings have been skilfully blended together to preserve an old atmosphere in Market Street. The steps of the old Town Hall which faces down the street can be seen on the extreme right of picture.

BARCLAYS INTERNATIONAL dominates the new Town Centre with the Sports Centre seen on the left. The Bus Station is left just out of the picture.

THE MODERN station slightly north of the old Victorian edifice is approached from the eastern side. The building top right opened in 1991 replaced the Junction Hotel which overlooked the old Station Approach. Note the modern (red, white and blue) livery on the sprinter train.

THE HOUSING estates which have grown up on the site of the old gasworks at Pitwines reach down to the harbour shore. These modern terraced residences have a fine view of the Fishermen's Dock and harbour.

AT THE bottom of the High Street the Scaplens Court, now restored as a museum, stands next to the Kings Head. Scaplens, dated 1536, was lovingly restored over many years by the Society of Poole Men. The King Charles Inn can be glimpsed in the background.

MARKET STREET leading to the old Town Hall has been lovingly preserved and gives visitors a chance of viewing old Poole.

ONE OF several merchants' houses which have survived and are dotted at various parts of Poole. This one, opposite the Parish Church, is West End House, the former residence of Robert Slade. The elegant new houses, left, are on the site of the Old Iron Foundry.